J   6257141
394.25   13.95
Vid
Vidrine
A Mardi Gras dictionary

DATE DUE			

A
MARDI GRAS
DICTIONARY

by
Beverly B. Vidrine

Illustrated by
Patrick Soper

SUNFLOWER PRESS

For my parents
BBV

Library of Congress Catalog Number 94-66951

ISBN 0-9641421-9-8

Printed in Hong Kong

Published by Sunflower Press
1000 Kim Drive
Lafayette, Louisiana 70503 U.S.A.

*T*he carnival of Mardi Gras takes place each year in New Orleans, Louisiana, and many other cities along the Gulf Coast in the United States of America. It is a season of fun and merrymaking.

AMERICAN INDIAN

(u•MER•I•kan IN•dee•un)

Groups of African-American men portray American Indians on Mardi Gras in their costumes covered with beads and feathers. The tradition of Mardi Gras Indians is over one hundred years old.

Ash Wednesday

(ash WENZ•day)

The day after Mardi Gras is Ash Wednesday, which begins the Christian season of Lent.

Balls

(bawlz)

During the weeks before Mardi Gras, carnival clubs have formal dances called balls. The king, queen, and their court are presented to the people who attend the balls.

Bands

(bandz)

Bands, or groups of people playing musical instruments, have marched in Mardi Gras parades since 1857.

eads

(beedz)

Beads, tiny pieces of plastic with holes through the center, are strung with thread to make necklaces. Mardi Gras float riders throw these colorful necklaces to the parade goers, who enjoy wearing all the beads that they catch.

Captain
(KAP•tun)

The captain is the person in charge of the carnival club or krewe.

Carnival
(KAHR•nuh•vuhl)

The word "carnival" comes from two Latin words that mean "to remove meat." This time of feast and festivity is followed by fasting during Lent.

Chickle-le-paw
(CHIK•l luh paw)

Many years ago, some children wore as costumes oversized pants stuffed with straw and shouted "Mardi Gras! Chickle-le-paw!" These American children had twisted the Creole words "<u>Tchou</u> <u>qu'</u> <u>a</u> <u>li</u> <u>paille</u>!" which mean "straw-stuffed bottom."

CAPTAIN

Colors
(KUL•urz)

Mardi Gras colors are purple, green, and gold. Purple is for justice, green for faith, and gold for power.

ostumes
(kos•TOOMZ)

A costume is clothing designed to picture a certain character. Some popular Mardi Gras costumes depict Indians, clowns, and gorillas. The people who wear costumes on Mardi Gras are known as "street maskers." Once a costume is selected, a street masker might say, "It's the real me!"

Courir du Mardi Gras
(KOO•rear duh mar•DEE graw)

"Courir du Mardi Gras," or the Mardi Gras Run, is a rural Mardi Gras celebration in southern Louisiana. Masked men wear patchwork costumes, capes, and peaked hats. They ride horses and stop at farmhouses to sing, dance, and beg for chickens. Later that day, the masked riders join their families and friends to enjoy a gumbo made from the chickens.

Debutante
(deb•ew•TONT)

A debutant is a young woman making her entrance into society. Some Mardi Gras krewes select debutantes to perform as maids in their courts. Usually these young women are relatives of krewe members.

Den
(den)

Float builders use large warehouses, or dens, to build and store the Mardi Gras floats.

Doubloons
(dub•LOONZ)

Doubloons, colorful coins specially made to celebrate the theme of each parade, are very popular Mardi Gras throws.

Easter
(EES•ter)

Easter is the feast of Christ's resurrection, or rising from the dead. Mardi Gras is always forty-six days before Easter.

ELKS ORLEANIANS
(elks AR•leen•ee•unz)

The Elks Orleanians is the oldest and largest of the truck krewes. This club and others ride in long, decorated flatbed trucks during the Mardi Gras truck parades. These truck riders throw doubloons, Mardi Gras Collector Cards, cups, and many other trinkets to the parade goers.

Expenses
(eks•PENS•es)

For parade goers, Mardi Gras is "The Greatest Free Show on Earth." Krewe members pay the expenses for the parades and carnival balls.

Fat Tuesday
(fat TOOS•day)

Fat Tuesday is a translation of the French words "Mardi Gras." This day ends the carnival season.

Flag
(flag)

Most Mardi Gras krewes have specially designed flags. These flags are given to the king and queen each year. Many purple, green, and gold flags are displayed during Mardi Gras at the homes of the past kings and queens.

FLOAT
(floht)

A Mardi Gras float, or a platform on wheels, is pulled by a tractor, and is decorated with a subject, or theme, chosen by each krewe. Colorful Mardi Gras floats, some as tall as buildings, carry costumed krewe members, or float riders, who throw doubloons, beads, and trinkets to the crowd.

Grandstand

(GRAND•stand)

During the Mardi Gras king's parade, the queen and her court stand on the grandstand, or raised platform, known as the queen's reviewing stand. It is a custom to stop the king's float at this point so he can greet the queen. Then during the queen's parade, the king and his court stand on the king's reviewing stand where they are greeted by the queen.

Holiday
(HOL•uh•day)

Mardi Gras is a holiday, or a day of freedom from work and school, in many cities that celebrate this special day.

Horn

(horn)

A horn is a musical wind instrument of brass. Some brass horns are trumpets, trombones, saxophones, tubas, and French horns. Many parade goers enjoy dancing to the band music played by the brass horns during Mardi Gras parades.

INSIGNIA

(in•SIG•nee•uh)

Many Mardi Gras throws, such as doubloons, have an insignia, or special mark, selected by the krewes to illustrate their theme.

January

(JAN•ew•air•ee)

January 6 is Epiphany, the twelfth day after Christmas. Traditionally this is the day that carnival begins.

JESTER

(JES•tur)

A jester performs with gaiety and merriment during many Mardi Gras balls to entertain the king, queen, and court.

KING

(king)

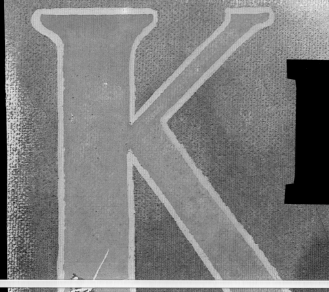

Most krewes select a member to rule as a make-believe king every Mardi Gras season. The king rides on a float in a special parade known as the king's parade. Then the king and his court preside over a ball in their honor.

King Cake
(king kayk)

A king cake is an oval ring of baked dough sometimes covered with icing and sprinklings of purple, green, and gold sugar. Hidden inside the cake is a tiny plastic doll. Traditionally, the person who finds the doll is "king" and gives the next king cake party.

Krewe
(kroo)

A Mardi Gras krewe is a carnival club or organization that plans the parades and balls. Some are children's krewes.

L**A**DDER

(LAD•er)

Some people carry a ladder with a seat built on top to the Mardi Gras parades. Children sit on these ladders so they can have a better view of the parades and catch more trinkets.

Lent
(lent)

Lent begins on Ash Wednesday and ends on Easter. Many Christians fast, or eat less food, to prepare for Easter.

Mardi Gras

(mahr•DEE graw)

In French, the word "mardi" means "Tuesday," and "gras" means "fat." On this last day of celebration of the festival season, many people wear costumes, watch parades, and attend balls.

Mardi Gras Comes To Louisiana

(mahr•DEE graw cumz too loo•ee•zee•AHN•uh)

A Frenchman named Iberville first celebrated Mardi Gras in Louisiana in 1699. He also named a bayou near the Mississippi River "Bayou du Mardi Gras."

MASK

(mask)

People wear masks to cover or hide their faces at Mardi Gras. Some might say, "I can dress up and be anything I want to be." Costumed adults and children have fun being someone different for a day.

New Orleans
(new AR•lee•unz)

The French founded the city of New Orleans.
Sometime later the people of New Orleans adopted the
French custom of celebrating Mardi Gras.

N I G H T   P A R A D E

(neyet puh•RAYD)

Some carnival krewes have traditional night parades.
Many floats are surrounded by torchbearers and
"flambeaux," or lighted torches, that light up the night.
Other floats have neon and running lights.

Ostrich PLUMES

(OS•trich ploomz)

The ostrich, a bird from northern Africa, has valuable wing and tail feathers, or plumes. Some Mardi Gras costumes are sewn with ostrich plumes. Many headdresses have ostrich plumes that are several feet high.

PARADE

(puh•RAYD)

A Mardi Gras parade has a theme, and the floats are decorated to illustrate the theme. The captain of the krewe leads the parade. Next come the krewe's officers, the king or queen, a title float, and the floats carrying costumed krewe members. Most floats are followed by clowns, marching bands, or dancers, who wind their way down the streets that are closed to traffic.

QUEEN

(kween)

Most krewes select a young woman to rule as a make-believe queen. Usually she is a krewe member's daughter, or granddaughter.

REX

(reks)

Rex, the name of a krewe in New Orleans, had the idea for the Mardi Gras colors (purple, green, gold) and the Mardi Gras flag. In 1960, the Krewe of Rex introduced a very popular throw, the doubloon.

cepter

(SEP•ter)

A scepter is a rod held by a ruler as a sign of authority. Mardi Gras kings and queens wave their scepters to the people who attend the parades and carnival balls.

Sharpe, H. Alvin

(sharp h AL•vin)

H. Alvin Sharpe, a skilled engraver, designed the first doubloon.

THEME

(theem)

A theme, or subject, is used in Mardi Gras parades and balls. Some themes have been children's stories, fairy tales, famous people, mythology, and history.

"Throw Me Something, Mister!"

(throh mee SUM•thing MIS•ter)

"Throw me something, Mister!" is the traditional street cry of the parade goers to the float riders. They want to catch and collect throws.

Throws

(throhz)

Gifts of trinkets, beads, Mardi Gras Collector Cards, and doubloons tossed by the masked float riders are known as throws. Many people have large collections of throws.

Tradition

(truh•DISH•un)

Tradition means the handing down of information, beliefs, or customs by word of mouth from one generation to another. The people who take part in Mardi Gras preserve it, or keep it alive, because of tradition. They are loyal to the past, and they appreciate ritual.

TRINKETS

(TRING•kets)

Trinkets are small ornaments, such as rings or bracelets. Plastic trinkets in many colors are thrown by the float riders to the crowd during Mardi Gras parades.

NIFORM

(EW•nee•form)

The marching band members are dressed alike with uniforms of the same design and color.

Venus

(VEE•nus)

The Krewe of Venus was one of the
many New Orleans Mardi Gras krewes.
The name Venus and many other
krewe names come from Greek, Roman,
and Egyptian mythology. Mythology is
a collection of stories or myths about
beliefs connected with religion.

WAVE

(wayv)

Parade goers crowd the streets and sidewalks
and wave their arms to and fro, hoping to catch
throws from the masked float riders.

(eks)

X is the number ten in Roman numerals. Most Mardi Gras kings and queens have a Roman numeral after their names. For example, the tenth Mardi Gras king had a Roman numeral X after his name (King Rex X).

(yell)

During Mardi Gras parades, excited people, especially children, crowd the streets. They leap into the air, stretch out their hands, and yell to the float riders, "Throw me something, Mister!"

ZULU

(ZOO•loo)

Zulu, an African-American Mardi Gras krewe in New Orleans, is named after an African tribe. The special Krewe of Zulu throw is the coconut.

Pronunciation Guide

Words in <u>A Mardi Gras Dictionary</u> are respelled to serve as a pronunciation guide. The accented syllables are in CAPITAL LETTERS in the respelling. This pronunciation guide is based on the following examples:

a, as <u>a</u> in <u>a</u>dd

ah, as <u>a</u> in f<u>a</u>ther

ai, as <u>ai</u> in <u>air</u>

ar, as <u>ar</u> in <u>arm</u>

aw, as <u>aw</u> in s<u>aw</u>

ay, as <u>a</u> in t<u>a</u>ke

e, eh, as <u>e</u> in <u>e</u>nd

ea, as <u>ea</u> in <u>ear</u>

ee, as <u>ee</u> in s<u>ee</u>d

er, as <u>er</u> in h<u>er</u>

ew, as <u>ew</u> in n<u>ew</u>

eye, y, as <u>i</u> in k<u>i</u>nd

i, ih, as <u>i</u> in w<u>i</u>n

o, as <u>o</u> in p<u>o</u>t

oh, as <u>o</u> in h<u>o</u>me

oi, as <u>oi</u> in <u>oi</u>l

oo, as <u>oo</u> in m<u>oo</u>n

ooh, as <u>oo</u> in f<u>oo</u>t

or, as <u>or</u> in f<u>or</u>

ow, as <u>ow</u> in <u>ow</u>l

s, as <u>s</u> in <u>s</u>ource, le<u>ss</u>

u, uh, as <u>u</u> in f<u>u</u>n

u, as <u>you</u> in <u>you</u>

ur, as <u>ure</u> in nat<u>ure</u>

ch, as <u>ch</u> in <u>ch</u>urch

sh, as <u>sh</u> in <u>sh</u>e

g, as <u>g</u> in <u>g</u>as

j, as <u>j</u> in <u>j</u>ump

th, as <u>th</u> in <u>th</u>ing

th, as <u>th</u> in <u>th</u>ere

z, as <u>s</u> in hi<u>s</u>